1 · 2 · 3
Church

Text by Gail Ramshaw

Art by Christine M. Winn

Augsburg

Minneapolis

Song and complete lyrics appear on last page.

1·2·3 CHURCH

Scripture quotations, unless otherwise noted, are from the New Revised Standard Version Bible © 1989 Division of Christian Education of the National Council of the Churches of Christ in the U.S.A. Used by permission.

Song: Mark Mummert
Cover design: Craig Claeys
Interior design: Circus Design

Library of Congress Cataloging-in-Publication Data

Ramshaw, Gail, 1947-
    1-2-3 church / text by Gail Ramshaw ; art by Christine M. Winn.
      p.   cm.
    Summary: Illustrations and rhyming text featuring numbers present
the essentials of Christian faith.
    ISBN: 0-8066-2335-7 (alk. paper)
    1. Christianity--Juvenile literature. 2. Children--Religious
life--Juvenile literature. 3. Counting--Juvenile literature.
[1. Christianity. 2. Counting.] I. Winn, Christine M., ill.
II. Title.
BR125.5.R36 1996
230--dc20 --dc20
[[E]]   96-35443
                                        CIP
                                        AC

Printed in Hong Kong   ISBN 0-8066-2335-7   10-23357

01 00 99 98 97 96 1 2 3 4 5 6 7 8

This book can be used in many ways. With parents and the Christian community, young children can count, read, and sing the mercies of God. But look carefully at each page! The number appears in more than one way. While the simple and engaging melody and rhymes help children and adults learn the essentials of Christian faith, the artwork tells a new story on every page. For instance, number One speaks of God, who creates, saves, and cares. Who is doing the creating, saving, and caring in the artist's image? How does God come to us in the church's worship? And, how do we continue to create, save, and care in the home?

Throughout the book, other words and images set forth the relationship between daily activities and what the church does at the Sunday liturgy. For instance, the first sacrament—baptism—appears on number Three. While three people play in the water, two other signs of baptism appear: the Christ-symbol of the fish splashing and the Trinity-symbol of a three-leafed shamrock. Who holds the shamrock and why is that creature sitting on a tree planted next to the water? Skip to number Seven and another baptismal image appears. At first it looks like a birthday party, but the image also speaks of the Spirit's gifts at baptism (what are they? See Isaiah 11:2) and hints at the church's birth at Pentecost (do you see the wind of the Spirit?). The second sacrament—eucharist—appears on number Two. Here we see a sister and brother in the kitchen with their two dogs. The young girl is taking a second loaf of bread out of the oven while her younger brother eats a slice of the freshly-baked bread. Do you notice the wall paper? How many twos can you find?

Other pages reveal stories of our spiritual ancestors. In number Five, we see a snake by a tree, animals on a boat, a boy with a many-colored coat, a pillar of fire passing through water, and a large mountain with light at the top. All five images are clues to five great stories: creation, flood, Joseph in Egypt, exodus, and Sinai. Number Four speaks of the four gospels. Can you name them? How is each gospel book different from the other?

Numbers Six, Eight, Nine, Twelve, Forty, and Fifty point toward the feasts and seasons of the year. What are the many meanings of the color that signals a new festival or season? Forty are the days of Lent that lead to the great Vigil of Easter represented at number Eight (the new fire, light of Christ, and the waters of baptism). Fifty continues the baptismal images of Lent and Holy Week with an Easter egg hunt set next to the sea and watched over by the Easter creatures. The weeks of Advent appear on number Nine where you will find a hint of the Advent wreath. Open Advent's door (turn the page) and the Twelve Days lead from Christmas (December 25) to Epiphany (January 6). Angels, shepherds, an "ox" and a "donkey," three young kings, the Epiphany star, and many trees fill the page. But can you find Mary, Joseph, and the newborn baby?

The final numbers become larger and larger! Open the Bible to the psalms and you will find new ways to speak of God, prayers for every day, and songs filled with gracious words. If young children are learning to pray simple prayers, they need to know that they can do so with hands open or closed or placed in a cross over the chest, with eyes open or shut, while standing, kneeling, sitting, resting in bed, or walking! And certainly the young child is not alone, but joined in baptism to millions of brothers and sisters in the faith. Yet all our counting will lead us to the great surprise that God's mercies are greater than any of our numbers.

Welcome, then, to this book of ordinary numbers that count the mercies of God.

One is our God

who creates, saves, and **cares.**

Two

is the bread and wine the church **shares.**

Three scoops of water,

and we are made **one.**

Four gospels tell

us the life of God's **son.**

Five books of Moses

show more of God's **grace**.

With one of **SIX** colors
we fix up our **space.**

The Spirit pours **seven** great gifts from **above.**

Eight
days in Holy Week

bring us God's **love**.

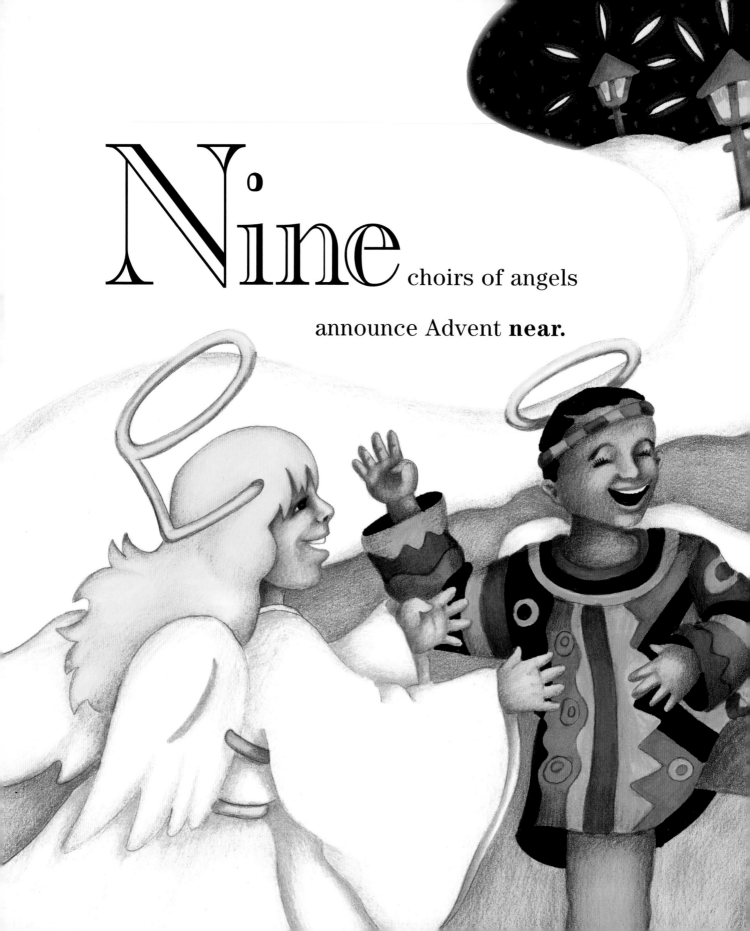

Nine choirs of angels

announce Advent **near.**

Twelve days of Christmas, and Epiphany's **here.**

Forty for Lent

when we wash away **sin.**

Fifty for Easter,

then Pentecost's **in.**

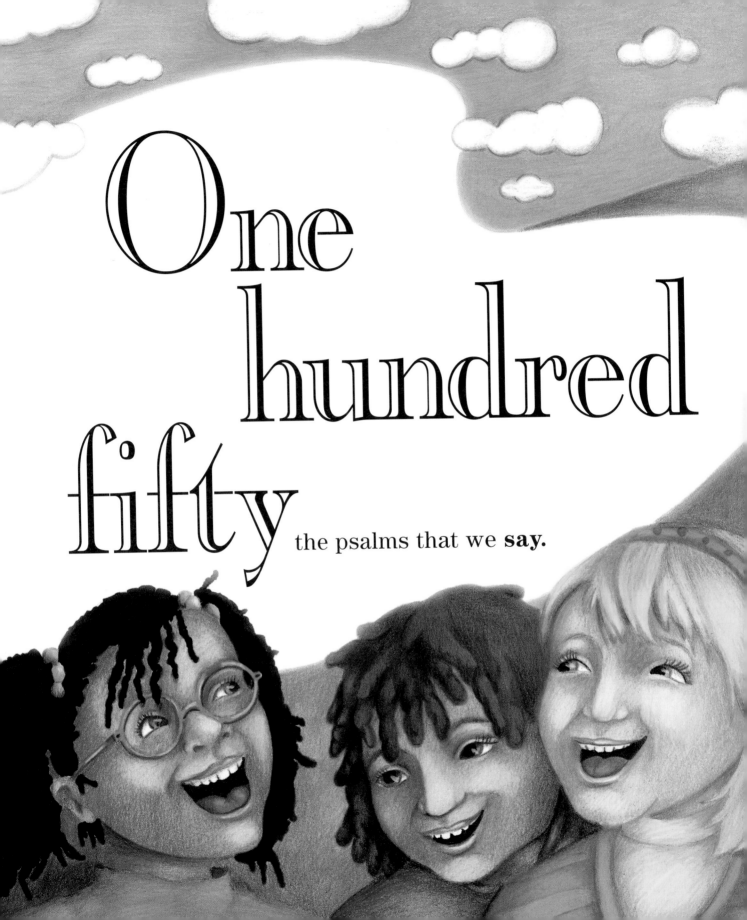

One hundred fifty the psalms that we **say.**

Thousands

of saints who join us to **pray.**

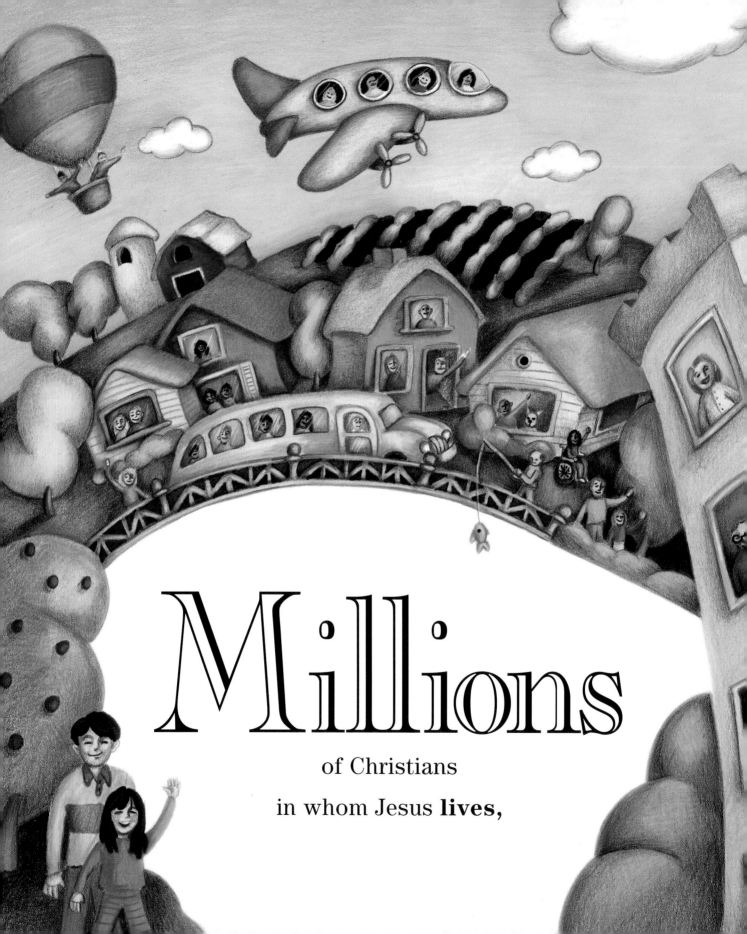

Millions

of Christians

in whom Jesus **lives,**

But numbers can't count
all the mercies God gives.

1·2·3 Church

Refrain

1 - 2 - 3, 1 - 2 - 3, 1 - 2 - 3 CHURCH! We're
count - ing the mer - cies of God._____ 1 - 2 - 3, 1 - 2 - 3,
1 - 2 - 3 CHURCH! We're count - ing the mer - cies of God.

Stanzas

1 *One* is our God, who cre - ates, saves and cares. *Two* is the
2 *Five* books of Mo - ses show more of God's grace. With one of *six*
3 *Nine* choirs of an - gels an - nounce Ad - vent near. *Twelve* days of
4 *One hun - dred fif - ty* the psalms that we say. *Thou - sands* of

bread____ and wine the Church shares. *Three* scoops of wa - ter and
col - ors we fix up our space. The Spir - it pours *sev - en* great
Christ - mas and E - piph - a - ny's here. *For - ty* for Lent when we
saints____ who join us to pray. *Mil - lions* of Chris - tians in

we are made one. *Four* gos - pels tell us the life of God's son.
gifts from a - bove. *Eight* days in Ho - ly Week bring us God's love.
wash a - way sin. *Fif - ty* for Eas - ter, then Pen - te - cost's in.
whom Je - sus lives, but num - bers can't count all the mer - cies God gives.

Text: Gail Ramshaw

Tune: Mark Mummert